# Wrap It Up
# for Kids

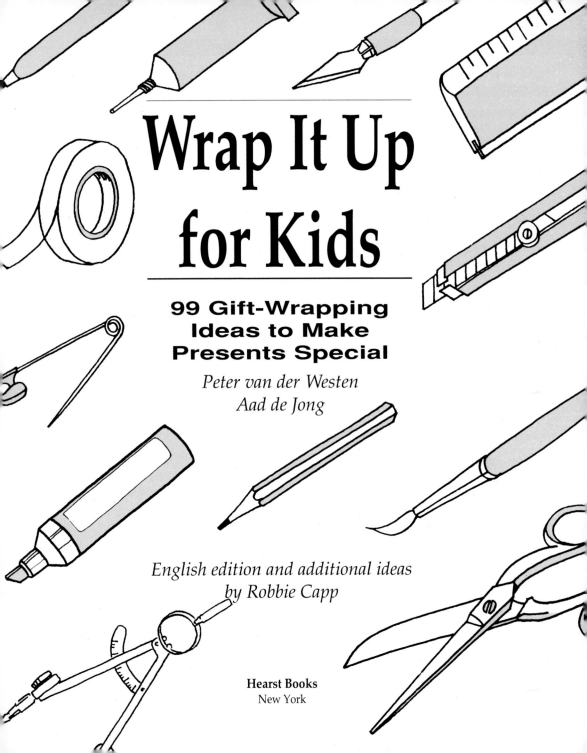

# Wrap It Up
# for Kids

## 99 Gift-Wrapping
## Ideas to Make
## Presents Special

*Peter van der Westen*
*Aad de Jong*

*English edition and additional ideas*
*by Robbie Capp*

**Hearst Books**
New York

Copyright © 1992 by Unieboek b.v.

Gift wrapping by Peter van der Westen and Aad de Jong, Verpakkingswinkel, Amsterdam
Creative organizations by Jack Botermans and Nicolette Botermans, Drimmelen
Illustrations by Dominique Ampe
Photography by Marga Rotteveel
Text by Tony Burrett
Dutch translation by Jaap van Teeckelenburgh

Published in the United States of America in 1992 by William Morrow and Company, 1350 Avenue of the Americas, New York, N.Y., 10019

First published in The Netherlands in 1992 by Unieboek b.v., PO Box 97, 3990 DB Houten, The Netherlands

ISBN 0-688-11209-9  LC 91-36039

Printed in Hong Kong

First Edition

1 2 3 4 5 6 7 8 9 10

BOOK DESIGN BY JACK BOTERMANS

# CONTENTS

# INTRODUCTION

When you give a present to a child, your pleasure is twofold: The fun of creating a charming package, and then enjoying the wide eyed delight that greets your effort. For few things excite a child more than receiving a gift – especially when it's imaginatively wrapped. And there are so many occasions for giving big and little gifts to children – not only on birthdays and holidays, but to reward good behavior, good marks on a test, good performance in the school play, or on the school team. Each occasion offers an opportunity to try your hand and ingenuity at creating packages (see page back, inside cover for a guide to gift-wrapping materials and tools) that are tailored to the event and the gift being given.

This book includes one kind of wrap for sports equipment – another for cuddly stuffed animals and still another for gifts of candy. The age of the boy or girl should also be taken into account when choosing wrapping materials and motifs. Bright primary colors – red, blue, yellow, green – always excite younger children, while teenagers can appreciate subtler, more offbeat color combinations such as lavender and lime green or turquoise and orange. Amusing paper patterns are widely available featuring famous cartoon characters, or try creating your own by cutting and pasting down panels from the Sunday comics page. Let the decorating theme and the size, shape, and colors of the package all give valuable clues to its content, to help children play that game they all love – guessing what's inside before they open it up.

It's true what they say about it being " the thought that counts". Especially when it comes to wrapping gifts for kids. Often they enjoy playing with the wrapping as much as with the gift itself. A little thought, time, and ingenuity in creating the wrap will go a long way in providing both giver and receiver with enjoyment well beyond the intrinsic value of the gift your wrap contains.

# WINGS-FOR-AN-ANGEL PACKAGE

This elaborate package combines variegated paper, bright tape, a multi bow on the side, and a multicolored, accordion-pleated bow mounted on top like soaring wings. The little angel you make this wrap for will surely delight over it as much as the gift it brings. The wrap was built up from separate lengths of paper carefully cut and pieced together. Lots of precision is needed to achieve this effect, but you may be lucky enough to find such a variegated pattern at a specialty paper shop. If not, use a single hot color in a high-gloss paper and concentrate your creativity on constructing the multicolored accordion wings.

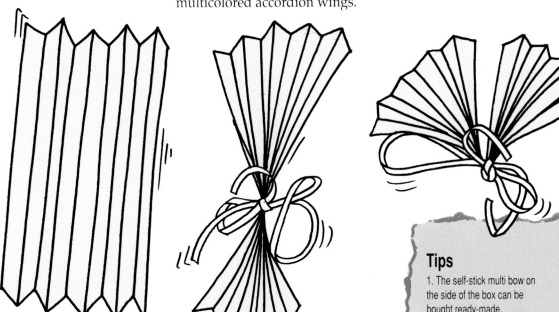

**How to Make Accordion Wings**

As an alternative to using ready-made multicolored paper, make your own by cutting strips of a few different colors and joining them with transparent tape. (The strips can be cut from any solid color paper – even construction paper, which comes many colors to a package.)

A. Make an accordion fold of your joined strips.

B. Pinch the center firmly and tie with a thin ribbon that matches one of the paper colors. Fan the accordion pleats and cut off their ends on a diagonal to form points.

C. Staple the accordion to the top of your package, and point the wings upward for a heavenly finish.

## Tips

1. The self-stick multi bow on the side of the box can be bought ready-made.
2. Instead of the multi bow on the side, substitute another accordion wing to double the heavenly effect.

9

# THE BONBON WRAP

This appealing wrap works best with small, rectangular boxes, a shape common to many popular gifts for children, such as miniature dolls or cars, or the latest rock hit on audiocassette. One end is puffed out to resemble a hard-candy wrapper. Called a toffee by the British and a bonbon by the French, in any language, this wrap is sure to please kids of all ages.

## How to Make the Bonbon Wrap

Cut a sheet of brightly patterned paper twice the length and width and three times the depth of the box to be wrapped. You'll need all this extra paper for overlapping and achieving the full puffed-out effect for one end of the box.

A. Place your box near one end of the sheet and wrap lengthwise in the conventional way.

B. Fold, crease, and tape one end.

C. Gather the paper at the other end and twist it tightly, keeping the paper puffed out, and tie the neck with a short piece of thin ribbon. Take three more

## Tips

1. Suit the paper pattern to the child's age.
2. Instead of mom wrapping the present for her child to take to a friend's birthday party, this easy wrap can be made by the child himself. What a good way to teach kids that it's a gesture of friendship to put time and thought into giftwrapping.

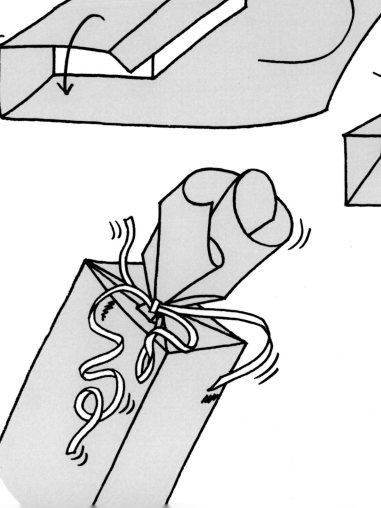

long pieces of thin ribbon of different colors and tie them together in a knot over your first knot. Use paper ribbon that can be curled when drawn firmly over a scissors blade.

11

# DOUBLE BONBON WRAP

Here's a two-ended version of the bonbon wrap on pages 11–12 this one made with tissue paper in two different colors. Another variation is a shoulder strap made from a long length of ribbon, so the package can be carried easily. After all, most kids can hardly wait to rush off and show a new gift to all their friends.

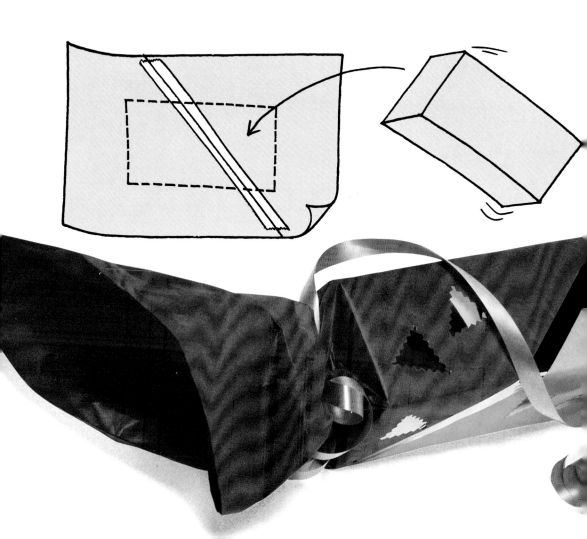

## How to Make the Double Bonbon Wrap

A. Start with two large pieces of tissue paper in contrasting colors. For strength, fold each over double, then fold each over again, this time on the diagonal, and join neatly along the seam with colored tape, as illustrated. Turn the sheet over and place your box in the center. Wrap lengthwise in the usual way and seal the ends with transparent tape.

B. Twist the ends and tie each neck with a short length of thin ribbon, and open the paper out in nice full puffs.

C. Cut a 5-foot (1.5 meters) length of medium-width curling ribbon. Tie a bow around the neck at one end, allow a 2 – 3-foot (60 – 90 cm) gap in the center, then tie a bow around the other end of the package. (For a taller child, of course, start with a longer length of ribbon for the shoulder strap.) Curl the trailing ends of the ribbon by drawing them firmly across a scissors blade.

### Tips.

1. This is the ideal way to wrap homemade chocolates or pre-packaged candies that come in a long oblong box.
2. You can animate a package wrapped in solid-colored paper by adorning it with decals. Adorable stickers come in a good variety of motifs.

## Tips

1. Decorate the side of the tube
with cartoon characters cut from
the Sunday comics, or bought
as self-stick decals.
2. Adapt this package to a
single, larger gift, such as a doll.
Replace the bird with a little
paper parasol mounted on a
longer stick.
3. Pick useful desk accessories
– scissors, ruler, pencils, pens –
wrap each separately in tissues
of different colors, and bunch
like a bouquet, sticking out of
the tube.

# THE LOLLIPOP PACKAGE

Since children delight so in opening gift wraps, you can really increase their pleasure by giving several small, related gifts, each wrapped separately and assembled in one enticing package. Especially designed for stick-shaped objects – lollipops, large paint brushes, big felt-tip markers – the package shown in the photo takes on still more charm with the whimsical bird-on-a stick ornament. All the items are put into a cardboard tube, with crumpled tissue or crepe paper and ribbons completing the lively look.

**How to Make the Lollipop Package**

A. Cut rectangles of crepe paper (or tissue doubled) about twice the length of the lollipops or other items to be wrapped.

B. Roll each up loosely and tie with narrow ribbon.

C. Insert the wrapped items into a cardboard tube, spreading them out to form a V. Add an ornament, something similar to the bird, tucked between the two lollipop packages.

D. The ribbon tails from the wrapped packages can be brought out of the tube to cascade over its side.

E. If needed to fill out the arrangement, extra tissue can be added at the top opening of the tube.

# THE COLORFUL CUBE WRAP

Prepackaged toys that come in cube-shaped boxes are good candidates for this cheerful wrap, which is made by putting a different color paper on each of the cube's six sides. Save cube boxes from foodstuffs and other commodities and use them to house small clothing gifts for kids, like socks, earmuffs, mittens, or rolled-up woolen scarves. You can also make a cube from scratch by simply taping together six same-size squares of cardboard.

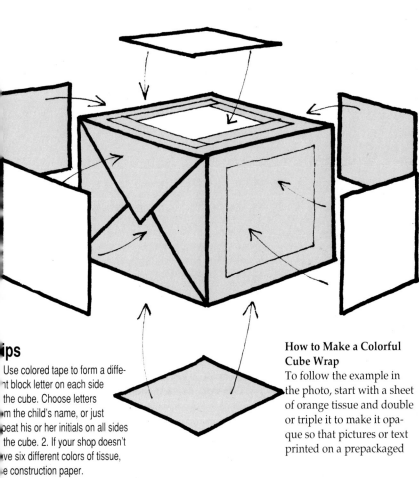

toy box won't show through. Then take six different bright colors of tissue paper, cut a square of each for each side of the cube. The size should be an inch or so (2 or 3 cm) smaller than the side of the cube. Position a square on the top of the cube and tape it in place as shown, using adhesive tape of a contrasting color. Affix the other squares to the other five sides in the same manner, using tape of a different color each time. A unified, symmetrical design will result by choosing tape and paper in identical colors, then alternating them on opposite sides of the cube. For example, if one side has purple paper and red tape, its opposite side would have red paper and purple tape. Alternate paper and tape colors on the other four sides in the same way: Team yellow and blue on one pair, green and white on the final sides.

**ips**

Use colored tape to form a diffe-nt block letter on each side the cube. Choose letters m the child's name, or just peat his or her initials on all sides the cube. 2. If your shop doesn't ve six different colors of tissue, e construction paper.

**How to Make a Colorful Cube Wrap**

To follow the example in the photo, start with a sheet of orange tissue and double or triple it to make it opaque so that pictures or text printed on a prepackaged

17

# THE SEEMINGLY SEAMLESS BOX

A sophisticated package such as this should be reserved for more expensive, "serious" gifts given to older children – perhaps a high-school graduation gift of a watch, a fine pen-and-pencil set, or a good calculator. The recipient will have to have a little patience to figure out how to open this package, since it's constructed in such a way as to be seemingly seamless.

**How to Make the "Seamless" Box**

A. Choose a thin, glossy cardboard in a color that complements the gift it's to contain. (Silver would be a good selection for a calculator, for instance.) On the reverse side of the cardboard draw the shape illustrated, following the suggested measurements and adjusting them if necessary to custom-fit your gift. With pencil, rule in the broken lines as shown, then cut out the whole shape using a hobby knife or sharp scissors. Score along the broken lines using the end of a large paper clip or a blunt knife, then turn the sheet over and complete the scoring on the glossy side. Another tool to use for scoring, if you have one on hand, is an empty ballpoint pen (but do make sure there's no ink in it).

B. Turn the cardboard over again and crease along the

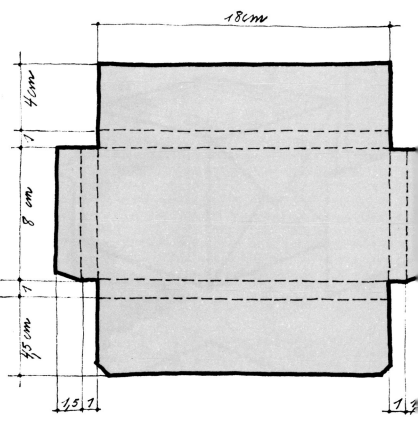

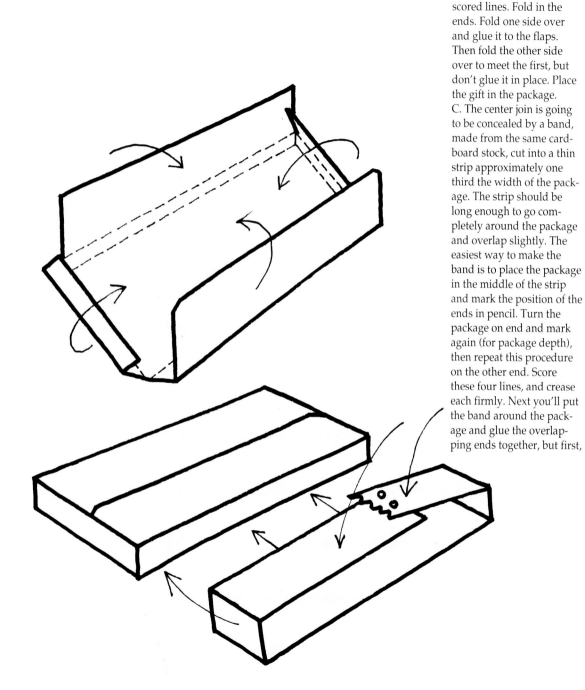

scored lines. Fold in the ends. Fold one side over and glue it to the flaps. Then fold the other side over to meet the first, but don't glue it in place. Place the gift in the package.
C. The center join is going to be concealed by a band, made from the same cardboard stock, cut into a thin strip approximately one third the width of the package. The strip should be long enough to go completely around the package and overlap slightly. The easiest way to make the band is to place the package in the middle of the strip and mark the position of the ends in pencil. Turn the package on end and mark again (for package depth), then repeat this procedure on the other end. Score these four lines, and crease each firmly. Next you'll put the band around the package and glue the overlapping ends together, but first,

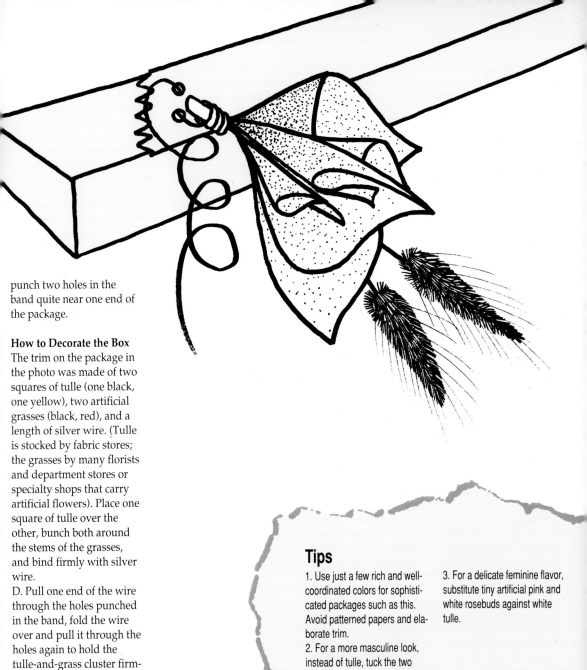

punch two holes in the band quite near one end of the package.

## How to Decorate the Box

The trim on the package in the photo was made of two squares of tulle (one black, one yellow), two artificial grasses (black, red), and a length of silver wire. (Tulle is stocked by fabric stores; the grasses by many florists and department stores or specialty shops that carry artificial flowers). Place one square of tulle over the other, bunch both around the stems of the grasses, and bind firmly with silver wire.

D. Pull one end of the wire through the holes punched in the band, fold the wire over and pull it through the holes again to hold the tulle-and-grass cluster firmly in place. The excess wire can be made into a spiral by coiling it around a pencil.

## Tips

1. Use just a few rich and well-coordinated colors for sophisticated packages such as this. Avoid patterned papers and elaborate trim.

2. For a more masculine look, instead of tulle, tuck the two grasses into a length of wide plaid ribbon doubled over to form a V.

3. For a delicate feminine flavor, substitute tiny artificial pink and white rosebuds against white tulle.

# HAVE A BALL!

If there's one gift category that spans all of childhood, from toddlers through teenagers, it's the ball in all of its forms. From the largest – beachballs, basketballs, volleyballs – to the smallest – baseballs, handballs, tennis balls – when a ball comes unboxed, it can be tricky to wrap. But here's a happy and colorful solution to the problem.

Carefully plan your size sheet of paper; it's always bigger than you might think when you're wrapping something round. The sheet shown here is intended for a soccer ball or medium-sized beachball of about a 24-inch (60 cm) circumference. The sheet measures 4 by 4 feet (1 square meter), so a good guideline is to make your paper twice the circumference of the ball to be wrapped.

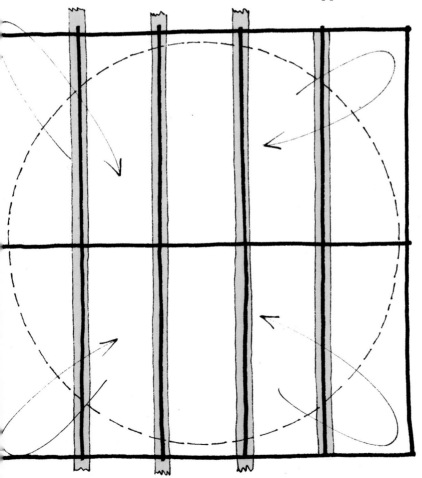

## How to Wrap a Ball

The multicolored wrap suggested here is an assemblage of ten tissue papers of different hues taped together (transparent or colored tape). Start with each sheet cut to 24 by 20 inches (50 by 40 cm), then for added strength, double each sheet over so that your working size is 24 by 10 inches (50 by 20 cm) per sheet.

A. Now lay the ten sheets out in two rows as shown, with the edges touching. Join all of the seams with tape. Cut off the corners of the sheet to form a circle (follow broken line on illustration).

B. Place the ball in the center of the circle, bunch your paper over it tightly, twist all the ends together into a neck, and tie with several lengths of shiny, thin ribbon, leaving long, trailing streamers.

# THE TAPERED BOX

This cute and useful box owes its inspiration to the take-out cartons widely used by Chinese restaurants. What an ideal package to contain small toys, puzzles, and games to take along on a family trip to keep the kids occupied in the back of the car. The tapered box can have anywhere from three to six sides, and by decreasing or increasing the length of the sides, can be shallow or deep, depending on gift content. The slope of the taper can also be adjusted by changing the angle between the sides and the base. Coloration is flexible, too: Make all sides one color, opposite sides different colors, or all sides different colors. Your final choice is whether to present the box closed or left open; and you can decorate it in a wide variety of ways.

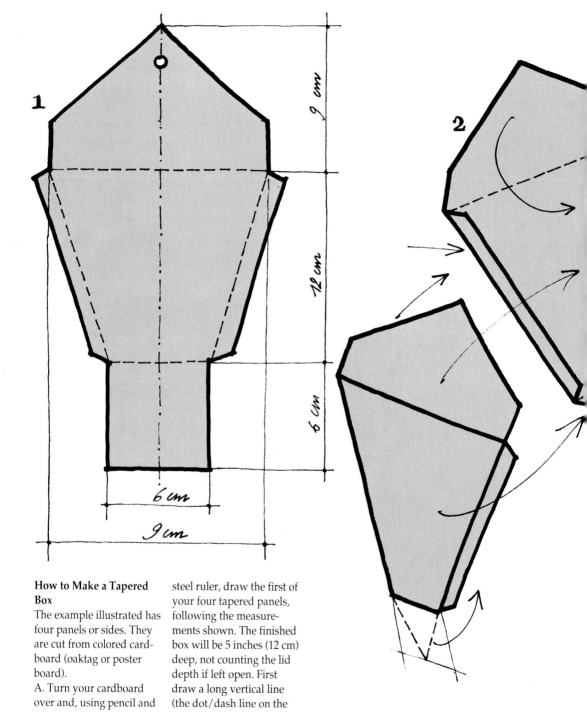

**1**

9 cm

12 cm

6 cm

6 cm

9 cm

**2**

## How to Make a Tapered Box

The example illustrated has four panels or sides. They are cut from colored cardboard (oaktag or poster board).

A. Turn your cardboard over and, using pencil and steel ruler, draw the first of your four tapered panels, following the measurements shown. The finished box will be 5 inches (12 cm) deep, not counting the lid depth if left open. First draw a long vertical line (the dot/dash line on the

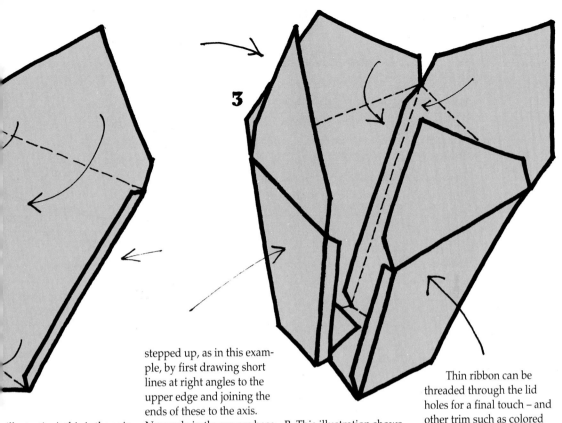

**3**

illustration); this is the axis and all other lines are drawn from it. Following the broken line, rule your base line (2 1/2 inches or 6 cm) at right angles to the axis and centered on it. Measure 5 inches (12 cm) above the base line and rule a 3 3/4-inch (9 cm) broken line at right angles to the upper edge of the panel. Join these lines. Rule in flaps on the two tapered sides (the heavy outline). Next, draw the lid, which can be either an equilateral triangle (three sides the same length), or can be

stepped up, as in this example, by first drawing short lines at right angles to the upper edge and joining the ends of these to the axis. Now rule in the square base (see Tip below for other base shapes). Draw three more panels in exactly the same way. Then with a hobby knife or sharp scissors, carefully cut out all four panels, following the heavy black lines on the illustration. Now score all the tapered sides (broken lines shown) using a ruler and a blunt knife or the end of a large paper clip, or if pressed lightly, a hobby knife, being careful not to cut through the cardboard. Bend the base and flaps inward and crease sharply.

B. This illustration shows how a three-sided box would be assembled. Fold the sides in and glue the flaps and base.
C. For a four-sided box, fold the sides in and glue; layer the four bases and glue together. The lids can be held closed with ribbon pulled through holes punched in each lid flap (see illustration A). Or leave the lid flaps open (as in the photograph), and conceal the gift content by loosely packing crumpled tissue or crepe paper or tulle inside the top of the open box.

Thin ribbon can be threaded through the lid holes for a final touch – and other trim such as colored plastic drinking straws, dried flowers, or a paper parasol can be added for further eye appeal.

## Tips

1. For the base of a three-sided tapered box, draw an equilateral triangle; for a five-sided box, rule a pentagon; and for a six-sided box, a hexagon. These shapes can be bought as plastic templates at an art-supply or variety store.
2. Homemade cookies or chocolates would be great fillers for the tapered box. Line it with wax paper or aluminum foil.

# TWOFERS:
## THE GIFT-IN-A-GIFT-PACKAGE

What delights a child more than receiving a gift? Receiving two –
one wrapped in the other. This clever wrap is actually a kite, in
which to conceal a second gift. Once that's removed, the kite can be
flown and enjoyed like any other. The kite wrap is ideal for gifts
that would usually be given in an envelope: money, a gift certificate,
baseball cards, tickets to a rock concert.

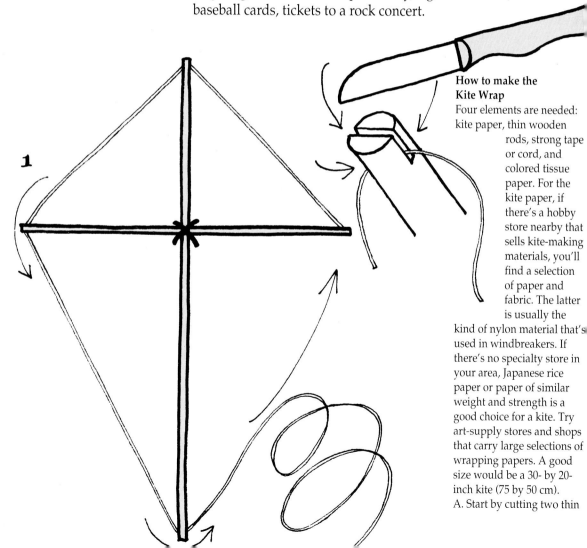

**1**

### How to make the Kite Wrap

Four elements are needed: kite paper, thin wooden rods, strong tape or cord, and colored tissue paper. For the kite paper, if there's a hobby store nearby that sells kite-making materials, you'll find a selection of paper and fabric. The latter is usually the kind of nylon material that's used in windbreakers. If there's no specialty store in your area, Japanese rice paper or paper of similar weight and strength is a good choice for a kite. Try art-supply stores and shops that carry large selections of wrapping papers. A good size would be a 30- by 20-inch kite (75 by 50 cm).

A. Start by cutting two thin

rods – a wooden dowel from a hardware store is perfect – one 30 inches, one 20 inches, and make a shallow notch in each end of both pieces.
B. Cross them and bind tightly in the center with tape or cord. With another length of cord, make a knot

securely where it joins the first knot you made.
C. Make a pattern for the kite shape (use newspaper), being sure that it's at least one inch (2.5 cm) larger all around than the kite outline given by the stretched cord. Lay the newspaper pattern on your kite paper; cut out your kite; then cut off the corners, as shown by the broken lines in the illustration.

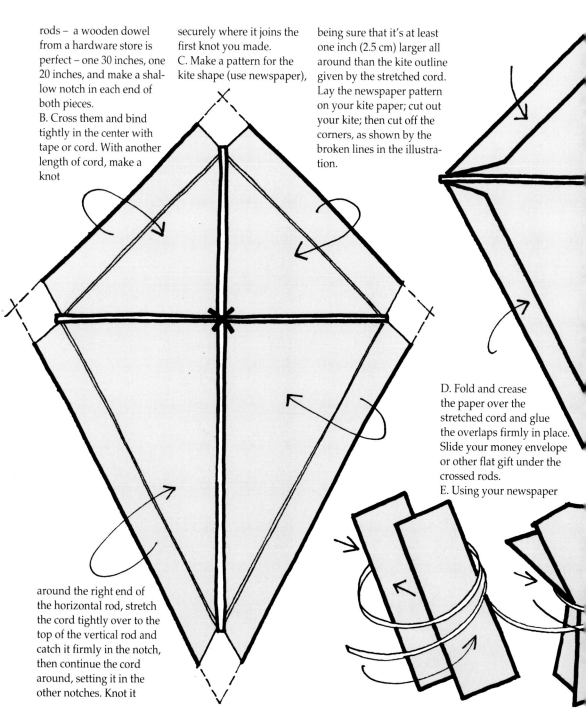

D. Fold and crease the paper over the stretched cord and glue the overlaps firmly in place. Slide your money envelope or other flat gift under the crossed rods.
E. Using your newspaper

around the right end of the horizontal rod, stretch the cord tightly over to the top of the vertical rod and catch it firmly in the notch, then continue the cord around, setting it in the other notches. Knot it

## How to Make the Kite Tail

F. Cut about a dozen pieces of brightly colored tissue paper, each piece 5 by 2 1/2 inches (12 by 6 cm) for the flat bow ties that will adorn the kite tail. Layer two tissues for each bow, pinch their centers, then knot the bows along a length of the same kind of cord as used for your kite outline, spacing the bows at regular intervals.

G. Decorate the front of the kite with a cute face made from colored stickers.

pattern again, cut another sheet of kite paper, but this time, slightly smaller than the kite itself. Position this sheet over the other, and glue all around the edges, sealing the gift envelope between the two sheets.

## Tips

1. The child receiving the kite may need help removing the gift inside without damaging the kite itself. If you've glued the backing sheet only around its edges, you should be able to remove it simply by inserting a long scissors blade through the liner at the center, then carefully cutting the back sheet away.

2. Professional artists use a glue called paper or rubber cement, stocked by art-supply stores. To remove paper glued with this product, a liquid thinner (which must be bought separately) is applied, and the glued sheets are peeled apart easily without the papers being damaged.

3. To fly the kite, you must attach a length of cord to its top and bottom corners. This should be long enough to reach almost arm's length to ensure that the kite is in balance when aloft. Attach a final long length of cord, as shown in the illustration, and your gift "wrap" is ready to take to the skies.

# WHAT A RACKET!

Just as it's hard to wrap a ball, it's hard to wrap a racket – especially since its shape is so obvious, and there's no mystery to the gift before it's unwrapped, so part of the fun is taken away from the child who loves to guess what's inside. Of course, you can always put a racket (or bat) into a big box, but if one isn't readily available, the best alternative is to make your nonmysterious wrap as bright and colorful as possible.

**How to Wrap a Racket**
Pick two really vibrant shades of tissue paper: orange and yellow, purple and lime green. Double each for extra strength. One should be somewhat longer than the racket handle, the other large enough to fold over its head completely (refer to photograph).
A. Join the sheets as shown,

using bright tape. Tear down one side, as shown in the illustration. Turn the sheet over and position the racket on it so that the neck is on the paper join. Fold the paper around the head, and tape; turn the sides of the paper toward the handle, fold around, and tape. Using curling ribbon, choose matching or still

other bright, contrasting colors, and wrap some long lengths of it around the racket neck, curling the ends by running them over a scissors blade tautly.

## Tips

1. If your gift includes a ball to go with the racket, wrap it as suggested earlier (page 23). Or, roll it up in the same color tissue used for the racket, then tape it all around in random crisscross fashion using a few different brightly colored tapes.

33

# THE ZIGZAG WRAP

Three "tricks of the trade" already described on earlier pages are combined here to make the zigzag wrap: It uses two sheets of different colors taped together; it has a deep pleat to create a banded effect; and the box is wrapped on the diagonal. All of these elements applied to one wrapping produces an inviting package that any child would be eager to receive. Use it to dress up a book, a box of paints, a videocassette, or similarly shaped gifts.

**How to Make the Zigzag Wrap**

Choose two sheets of patterned or solid-colored wrapping papers that mix well.

A. Cut each sheet on the diagonal, as illustrated, and join the seam with colored tape – gold is a sophisticated choice.

B. Make a deep pleat down the center by folding and firmly creasing the paper, as illustrated.

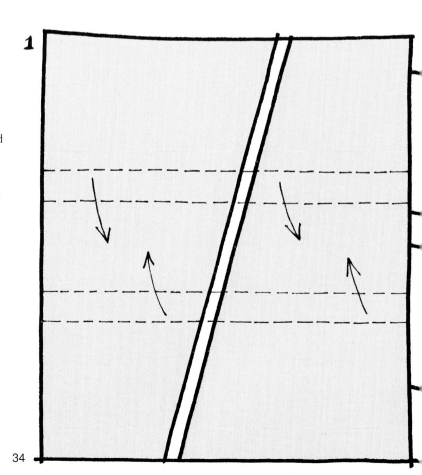

**2**

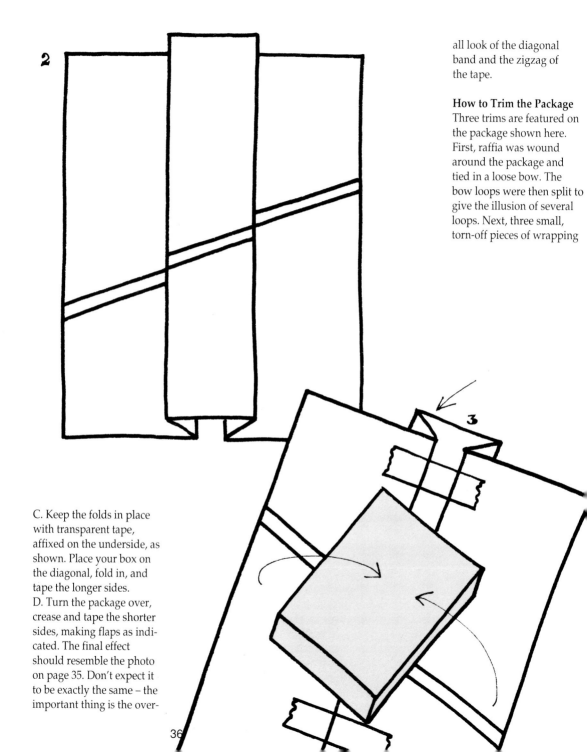

all look of the diagonal band and the zigzag of the tape.

**How to Trim the Package**
Three trims are featured on the package shown here. First, raffia was wound around the package and tied in a loose bow. The bow loops were then split to give the illusion of several loops. Next, three small, torn-off pieces of wrapping

**3**

C. Keep the folds in place with transparent tape, affixed on the underside, as shown. Place your box on the diagonal, fold in, and tape the longer sides.
D. Turn the package over, crease and tape the shorter sides, making flaps as indicated. The final effect should resemble the photo on page 35. Don't expect it to be exactly the same – the important thing is the over-

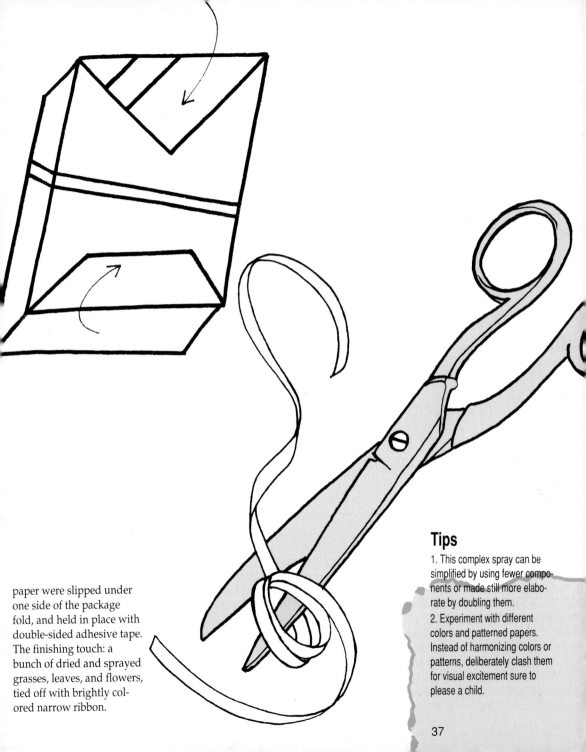

paper were slipped under one side of the package fold, and held in place with double-sided adhesive tape. The finishing touch: a bunch of dried and sprayed grasses, leaves, and flowers, tied off with brightly colored narrow ribbon.

## Tips

1. This complex spray can be simplified by using fewer components or made still more elaborate by doubling them.

2. Experiment with different colors and patterned papers. Instead of harmonizing colors or patterns, deliberately clash them for visual excitement sure to please a child.

# THIS WRAP FITS TO A "T" !

The mainstay of most children's wardrobes these days is the T-shirt. They never seem to have too many, and always welcome more as gifts. When you wrap a T-shirt – or sweat shirt, pajamas, or other clothing gifts boxed by the store – you can dress up the gift by adding a few unusual yet simple touches, as shown here, turning a conventional wrap into an eye-catching presentation.

### How to Make the T-Shirt Wrap

A. Take a sheet of colored tissue and make a double fold down one side, as indicated by the broken lines in the illustration. Place your box on the opposite end of the paper, as in the sketch, and wrap it lengthwise, following the arrows. Check to see that the fold lies roughly in the position shown.

B. Instead of making V-folds, close the short ends of the package with a straight double fold and seal with tape or, as in the photo, a round sticker over the edge on each end. Using another color paper (red in photo), cut a strip shorter than the package width and four times as wide as the (light blue) fold. Fold the strip in half lengthwise, crease firmly, slip under the fold, and seal with three round stickers.

## Tips

If using tissue paper, the sheet may not be large enough to go around a clothing box, in which case, join two sheets with transparent tape.

# OVER THE RAINBOW

The best shape for this wrap is a deep, oblong box that holds a doll, truck, car, construction set, or other toy. A rainbow of bright colors should be chosen for younger children, while older girls and boys can appreciate subtler shades such as pastels or many gradations of one color for a monochromatic look.

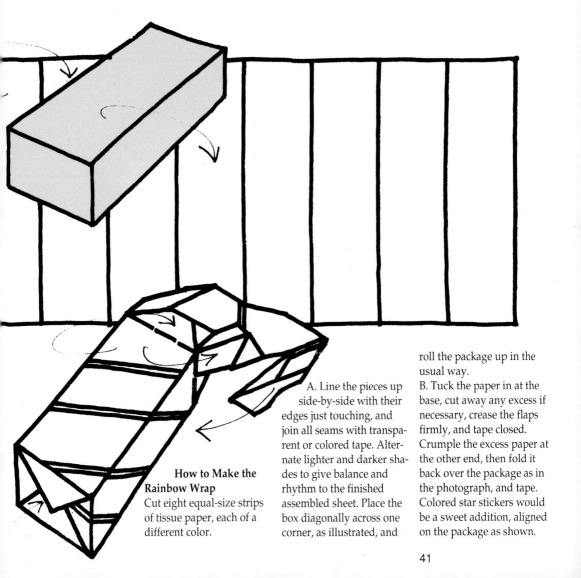

**How to Make the Rainbow Wrap**
Cut eight equal-size strips of tissue paper, each of a different color.

A. Line the pieces up side-by-side with their edges just touching, and join all seams with transparent or colored tape. Alternate lighter and darker shades to give balance and rhythm to the finished assembled sheet. Place the box diagonally across one corner, as illustrated, and roll the package up in the usual way.

B. Tuck the paper in at the base, cut away any excess if necessary, crease the flaps firmly, and tape closed. Crumple the excess paper at the other end, then fold it back over the package as in the photograph, and tape. Colored star stickers would be a sweet addition, aligned on the package as shown.

# THE TISSUE-TWIST WRAP

Combining papers of two different weights and textures gives this package a special twist – literally and figuratively. Tissue paper is color coordinated and joined to a patterned paper, then bunched, twisted, and draped over the front of the package to form a sort of cravat or scarf. What an appropriate wrap for a gift of a shirt, blouse, or sweater to a teenage boy or girl.

**How to Make the Tissue-Twist Wrap**

First select a lively patterned paper, then a tissue that matches the design's dominant color. Your sheet of patterned paper should be as long as the package and twice as wide, plus twice the thickness and a little extra for overlap.

A. Cut one end diagonally, as shown. Double your tissue paper and cut a sheet the same width as the patterned paper, but at least half again as long. Cut it on the diagonal and join the two papers with colored tape (of another tone found in the pattern – or perhaps a neutral – gold, silver, or black). Turn the paper over and place your box on top of the paper seam.

B. Fold the longer sides over and tape; fold the patterned-paper end over, crease, and tape. Flatten out the tissue end, bunch gently at the neck, and twist into shape. Fold over to the front of the package, and secure with a spot of glue or two-sided tape.

## Tips

1. Instead of patterned paper, choose a high-gloss solid-colored paper – a brilliant red joined to hot-orange tissue with shiny black tape. Then decorate the lower right corner of the box with black tape cut out to form block letters of the child's initials ( a "monogram" to go with the "cravat").
2. As a clue to the shirt or blouse gift inside, glue some little white buttons down the front of the package – again, more effective on solid, rather than patterned, paper.

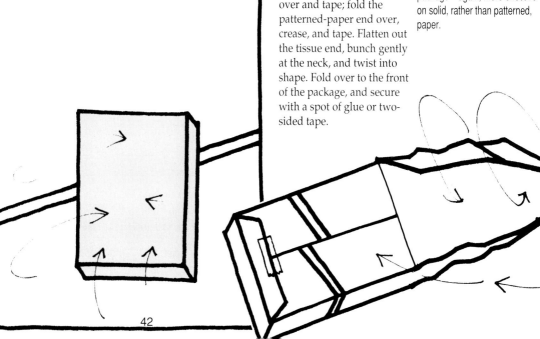

# THE DOMINO WRAP

This crisp-looking black-and-white wrap is meant to look like a large domino, and is easier to make than you might think on first looking at the photo. A variation on the "seamless" wrap on page 18, instead of the paper closing the usual way on the surface of the package, the join is along one of its shallow sides, and, if sealed carefully, will not be apparent. With both front and back surfaces completely seamless, the addition of round stickers, appropriately placed, creates the domino look-alike.

Any item that is packed in a flat box is a candidate for this wrap: books, a compact camera, watercolor set, jigsaw puzzles, and, of course, a box of dominos – concealed in a larger box.

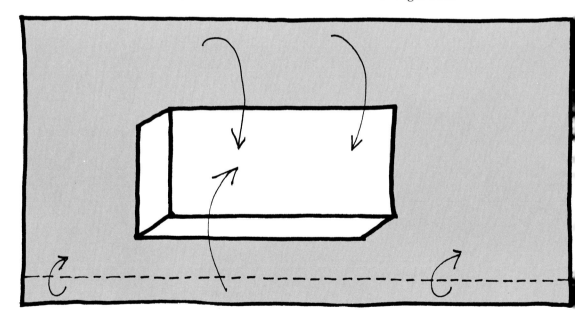

**How to Make the Domino Wrap**

Glossy black paper is perfect for this wrap. It might also be made of tissue, probably doubled for strength – and it could be white instead of black. Because the joins are on the sides, the measurements must be precise (see Tip below): The length should be equal to the box length plus six times its thickness (three times its thickness at each end to allow for folding). Its width should be twice the width of the box plus one-and-a-half times its thickness (to go completely around the package, plus a little overlap along one side).

A. Place the box on your cut

sheet of paper, as shown in the sketch. Following the arrows, wrap the box lengthwise so that the two sides overlap along the box side. Secure with a length of double-sided tape placed between the overlap.

B. Fold each end into a triangle and crease firmly.

C. Fold over the point of each triangle, then fold again.

D. Use double-sided tape to seal.

**How to Make the Domino Trim**

Assuming you've started with black paper, you'll need white tape and several round white stickers to simulate the white domino dots, or black tape and stickers, if your wrapping paper is white. (See Tips below.)

E. Across the center of the top surface of your package, place a thin strip of tape of the same color – white or black – as the dots. Also make an L and place it in each corner, as shown. Repeat this design on the underneath surface. In placing the domino dots, refer to actual dominoes for correct positioning before affixing them to the paper. For a final trim of ribbon, take several lengths of colored twines and wrap them around the sides of the box, ending them in a large bow.

## Tips

1. If you can't find ready-made white stickers, make your own by cutting them from white self-stick mailing labels. Use a circle template (which offers a range of circle sizes) and pencil all your circles in first, then cut them out with a

cuticle scissors (the curve and small size of this scissors facilitates round cutting).

2. If it's a birthday gift, have the domino dots add up to the child's age.

3. Since the paper needs to be cut precisely for a "seamless" join, you might test the size first with newspaper, then use that for your pattern before cutting into you good wrapping paper.

# THE HARLEQUIN WRAP

Bright triangles pieced together at one end and a tissue puff at the other give this wrap a jaunty, harlequin look. The larger and more multicolored the triangles, the greater the impact – so save this idea for fairly big packages – shoebox-size at least. In fact, if your gift item isn't prepackaged, a shoebox is a terrific container for it; for example, dolls or dumptrucks for toddlers; an assortment of arts-and-crafts materials for the six-to-twelve-year-old set; paperback books or video games for teenagers.

## How to Make the Harlequin Wrap

There are seven different tissue colors in the photographed package, but you can use fewer or more. First, to determine the size of the total sheet you'll need, wrap a piece of newspaper around your box, then use it as a pattern for the tissue you'll now cut.

A. Choose three different colors of tissue paper, double each sheet for added strength, then cut equal oblong pieces. Align them as shown and join their seams with colored tape. To prepare for your next step – cutting triangles from four other colors of tissue (also doubled) – first cut a triangle pattern from newspaper.

B. Prepare two triangles for each of two oblong panels. Each triangle base should be half the width of the oblong, its height more than halfway up the sheet, as shown. Position the triangles side-by-side and glue or tape (double-sided) in place. With the third oblong panel to the left, tear off the edge as shown.

C. Turn the sheet over and place your box on a diagonal. Fold, crease, and tape the longer sides in the usual way.

D. Fold the corners of the package base to form a long triangle, then fold it over and close with transparent tape. Bunch the paper at the other end and twist into a neck. Tie with colored ribbon, yarn, or twine.

49

# THE TEDDY BEAR WRAP

Cuddly toy animals are not only popular with toddlers. They're often collected by older children and even teenagers love to decorate their rooms with them and enjoy receiving more to add to the menagerie piled up on their beds. But, like balls, stuffed toy animals are tricky to gift wrap. Try this distinctive and cheerful solution – a multicolored wrap that conveys the cuddliness of its contents. As with package styles on some earlier pages, this wrap is made of different papers taped together into one large sheet. While the sizes of furry toy animals vary widely, the example shown here is a medium-sized teddy bear, wrapped in a sheet of 32 by 38 inches (about 50 by 95 cm).

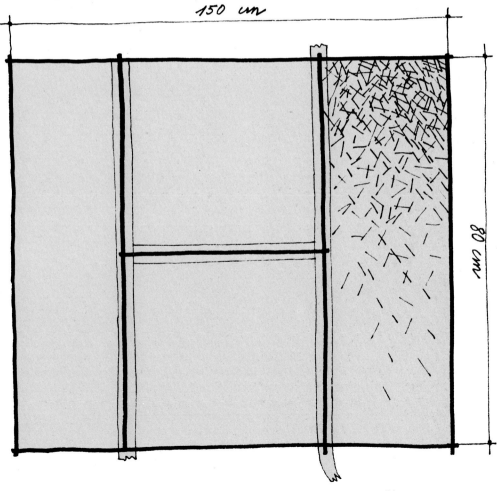

## How to Make the Teddy Bear Wrap

Use tissue paper in four different colors, each sheet doubled.

A. Cut two squares and two oblongs of the approximate measurements shown. Give a textured effect to one oblong by crumpling it up, then flattening it out again (as indicated on right panel, which will be the top of the package when wrapped). Join the three seams with silver tape.

B. Position the bear as shown, and fold the bottom two corners so that they meet at the bear's head. Join with transparent tape.

C. Now fold the bottom point up and tuck in – rather like diapering a baby!

D. Fold the sides of the sheet over loosely and tuck in, leaving enough paper free to form the package head.

E. Just above the bear's head bunch the paper together and twist it, then tie several times around with thin ribbon or twine. If you've used curling ribbon, finish off the ends by pulling it across a scissors blade to make spirals.

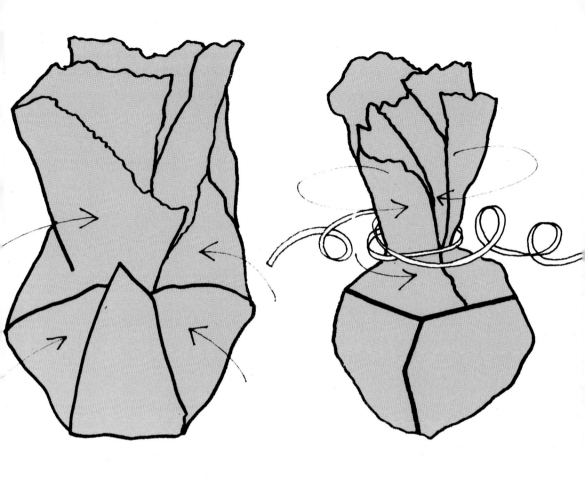

## Tips

1. Decorate your package with cute little animal decals.
2. Instead of ribbon, take remnants of knitting yarn and twist them into a multicolored length to tie up and bow your package.

# THE WINDOWED PYRAMID BOX

When a gift is small but costly – such as a fine miniature car or a good watch – you can emphasize the importance of the child handling the gift with care by presenting it in a special, carefully constructed box. This easy-to-make, one-piece pyramid is just the thing, and it even has a window for previewing the exciting gift inside.

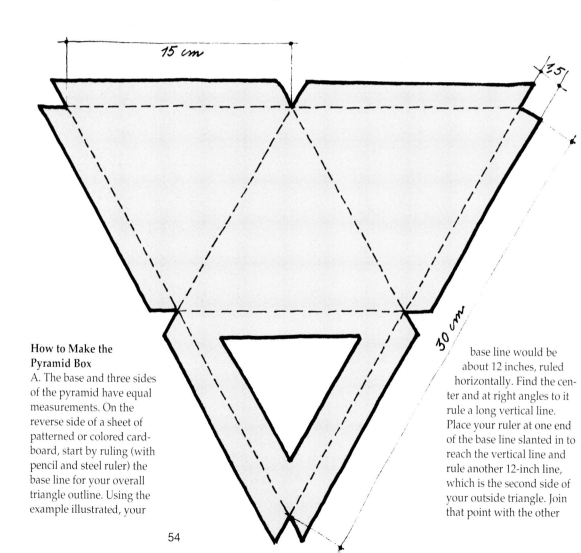

**How to Make the Pyramid Box**

A. The base and three sides of the pyramid have equal measurements. On the reverse side of a sheet of patterned or colored cardboard, start by ruling (with pencil and steel ruler) the base line for your overall triangle outline. Using the example illustrated, your base line would be about 12 inches, ruled horizontally. Find the center and at right angles to it rule a long vertical line. Place your ruler at one end of the base line slanted in to reach the vertical line and rule another 12-inch line, which is the second side of your outside triangle. Join that point with the other

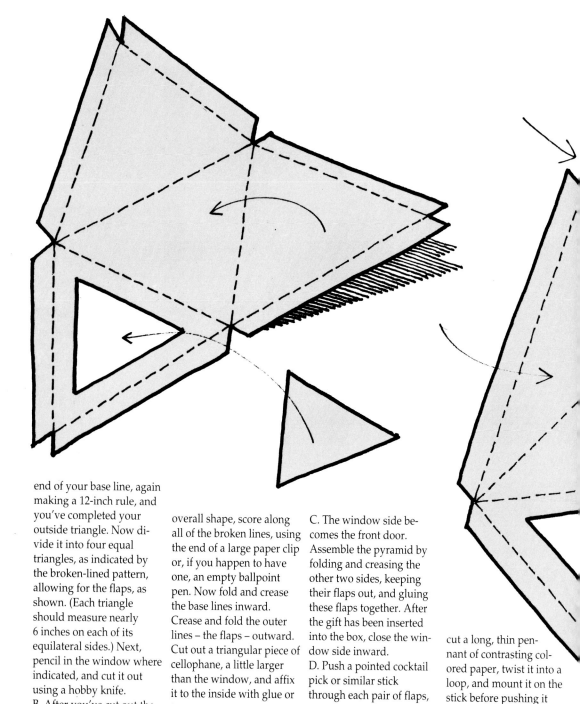

end of your base line, again making a 12-inch rule, and you've completed your outside triangle. Now divide it into four equal triangles, as indicated by the broken-lined pattern, allowing for the flaps, as shown. (Each triangle should measure nearly 6 inches on each of its equilateral sides.) Next, pencil in the window where indicated, and cut it out using a hobby knife.

B. After you've cut out the overall shape, score along all of the broken lines, using the end of a large paper clip or, if you happen to have one, an empty ballpoint pen. Now fold and crease the base lines inward. Crease and fold the outer lines – the flaps – outward. Cut out a triangular piece of cellophane, a little larger than the window, and affix it to the inside with glue or transparent tape.

C. The window side becomes the front door. Assemble the pyramid by folding and creasing the other two sides, keeping their flaps out, and gluing these flaps together. After the gift has been inserted into the box, close the window side inward.

D. Push a pointed cocktail pick or similar stick through each pair of flaps, as shown. For added flair,

cut a long, thin pennant of contrasting colored paper, twist it into a loop, and mount it on the stick before pushing it through the flaps.

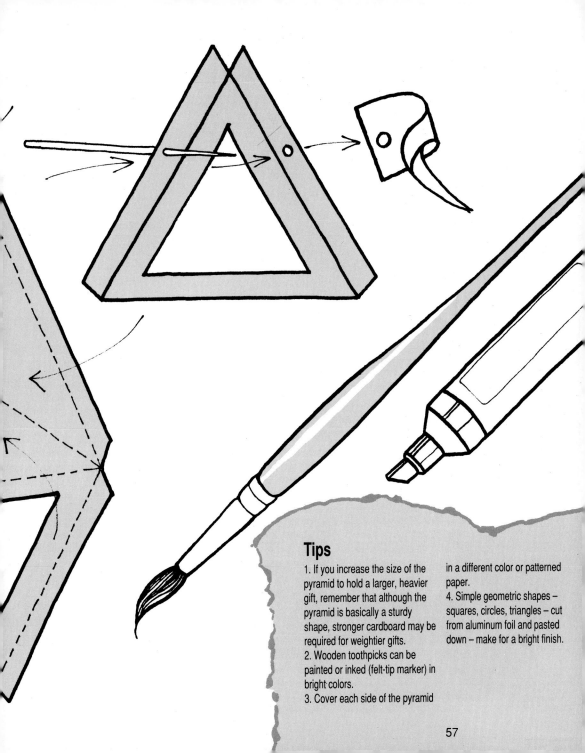

## Tips

1. If you increase the size of the pyramid to hold a larger, heavier gift, remember that although the pyramid is basically a sturdy shape, stronger cardboard may be required for weightier gifts.

2. Wooden toothpicks can be painted or inked (felt-tip marker) in bright colors.

3. Cover each side of the pyramid in a different color or patterned paper.

4. Simple geometric shapes – squares, circles, triangles – cut from aluminum foil and pasted down – make for a bright finish.

57

# THE DIAMOND BOX

This gem of a package is easier to make than it appears to be. Instead of constructing the corners at right angles, as you would with a square box, you adjust your measurements a bit and create an almost diamond-shaped, two-piece box that's perfect for holding individually wrapped hard candies (see further suggestion under Tips).

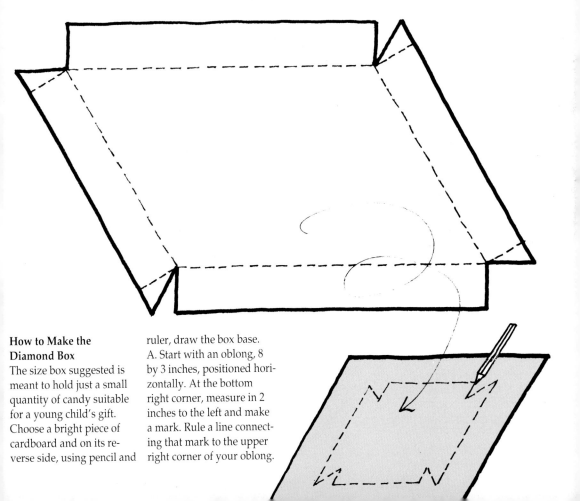

## How to Make the Diamond Box

The size box suggested is meant to hold just a small quantity of candy suitable for a young child's gift. Choose a bright piece of cardboard and on its reverse side, using pencil and ruler, draw the box base. A. Start with an oblong, 8 by 3 inches, positioned horizontally. At the bottom right corner, measure in 2 inches to the left and make a mark. Rule a line connecting that mark to the upper right corner of your oblong.

Now go to the upper left corner of your oblong and measure in 2 inches, make a mark, and rule a line from there to the lower left corner of your oblong. Your diamondlike shape should match the heavy outline in sketch A, with horizontal sides measuring 6 inches and being exactly parallel to each other, and the slanted sides measuring 3 1/2 inches and being exactly parallel to each other.

B. Following the broken lines, which are 1/2 inch in from the edge of the diamond outline, prepare your score lines. Now cut out your whole diamond shape (the heavy outline in sketch A). Using it as a template for your box lid, turn your diamond over, lay it on the reverse side of a second piece of cardboard, and draw around the whole shape. Cut it out. Pencil in score lines, making them 1/2 inch in from the outside of the diamond. Now make a cut in all the corners of both base and lid, as shown in sketch B.

C. Since the lid should be shallower than the base, trim a little off the sides – about 1/8 inch all around. (The base is 1/2 inch deep, the lid 3/8 inch deep.)

D. Now score both base and lid along broken lines. Use a steel ruler and a hobby knife (but be careful not to cut through the cardboard);

other good scoring tools are the end of a large paper clip or an empty ballpoint pen. Crease all sides firmly, fold in, and glue or tape the flaps to the insides of adjacent sides.

## Tips

1. Take individually wrapped, flat, hard candies and stick them along a length of colored tape to go inside your diamond gift box.
2. Adapt the diamond-shaped box to larger sizes for holding all kinds of children's gifts. For instance, double the size of the diamond just described and make it much deeper, and you'll have a terrific gift box for colorful tights for a little girl, or tube socks for a boy.
3. Run a wide satin ribbon around the box, tie in a simple overhand knot, leave long ends and spread them out almost to reach the sides of your box, then cut the ends into deep points to harmonize with the diamond motif.

# CASE IN POINT

A pointed, four-sided box is just the thing to encase an upright gift: a jar of bubble bath, a small doll or toy soldier, a little sailboat. The size is easily adjusted by enlarging or reducing the dimensions of the square base and four triangular sides.

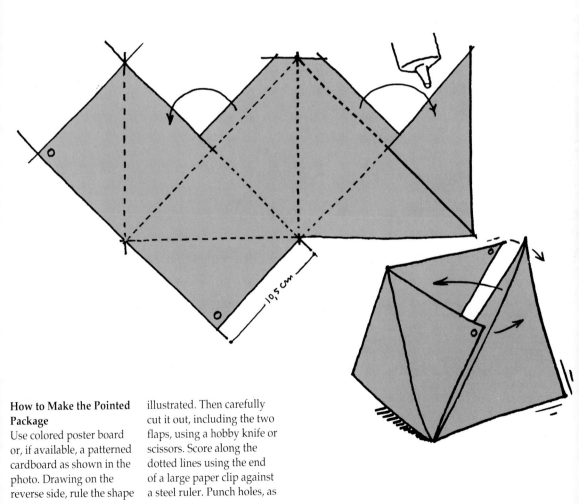

**How to Make the Pointed Package**
Use colored poster board or, if available, a patterned cardboard as shown in the photo. Drawing on the reverse side, rule the shape illustrated. Then carefully cut it out, including the two flaps, using a hobby knife or scissors. Score along the dotted lines using the end of a large paper clip against a steel ruler. Punch holes, as

shown in the sketch, then fold and crease the cardboard inward along the scored lines, fold the shape together, and glue the flaps to their appropriate sides.

After inserting the gift, close the box, fold the two halves together, thread a length of ribbon or thin colored cord through the holes and knot, then finish off with a bow and long streamers, as depicted.

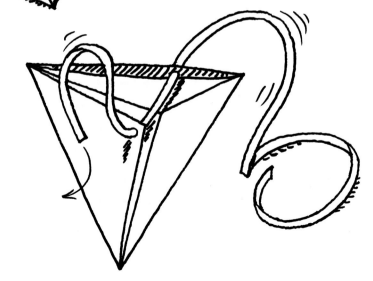

## Tips

1. Since the pyramid is a strong shape, if made of thicker or doubled cardboard, it will support heavier objects.

2. If you'd like a patterned design and can't find it in heavy stock, use plain poster board and cover it with patterned paper before drawing and cutting out the shape.